There is no one method or technique that is the ONLY way to learn to read. Children learn in a variety of ways. **Read with me** is an enjoyable and uncomplicated scheme that will give your child reading confidence. Through exciting stories about Kate, Tom and Sam the dog, **Read with me**:

- *teaches the first 300 key words (75% of our everyday language) plus 500 additional words*

- *stimulates a child's language and imagination through humorous, full colour illustration*

- *introduces situations and events children can relate to*

- *encourages and develops conversation and observational skills*

- *support material includes Practice and Play Books, Flash Cards, Book and Cassette Packs*

Always praise and encourage as you go along. Keep your reading sessions short and stop immediately if your child loses interest.

Ladybird books are widely available, but in case of
difficulty may be ordered by post or telephone from:

Ladybird Books – Cash Sales Department
Littlegate Road Paignton Devon TQ3 3BE
Telephone 01803 554761

A catalogue record for this book is available
from the British Library

Published by Ladybird Books Ltd Loughborough Leicestershire UK
Ladybird Books Inc Auburn Maine 04210 USA

Read with me
The robbery

by WILLIAM MURRAY
stories by JILL CORBY
illustrated by TERRY BURTON

Tom and Kate were at home playing games with their toys. They were cleaning Kate's dolls' house. When the dolls' house was clean, they put all the things back in it.

"It will soon be Christmas," Kate told Tom. "What would you like for Christmas, Tom?"

"I would like a police car and a police van," he said. "If I had a police car and police van, I could play many more games."

"I like playing games as well," Kate said. "That's what I would like, a new game that we could all play. I don't want any more dolls."

Their mother could hear what they were saying. "You should think about the presents that you would like to give to others as well," she told them, "not just about things you would like to have for Christmas. We will have to go to the shops soon and buy our Christmas presents."

When Kate saw her mother on her own, she said, "I know what Tom would like for Christmas, a police car and a police van."

The next morning they got ready to go to the shops. They went to the bus stop and waited for the bus to come. They waited quite a long time and it started to rain.

"It looked like rain this morning," Mum said.

"We are going to get wet if this rain goes on," Kate said.

Then Tom saw the bus coming, and they all got on. Mum got the tickets and they sat down at the back of the bus.

"We are not very wet," Tom said. "The bus came just in time."

"Sam likes riding on a bus, so he is always good," Kate said to her mum. "And he is not very wet."

Sam sat by Tom and they looked at everyone on the bus. The rain had made some of them very wet.

Soon they were at the shops so they all got off.

Mum said that Tom could buy his Christmas present for Kate first. So Kate had to wait outside the shop with Sam, while Tom and Mum went inside.

Sam sat and waited with Kate by the shop window. They looked in the window.

It looked very nice, with Father Christmas with his big bag on his back. Kate started to count the presents that she could see.

"One, two, three, four, five. I can count five presents," she told Sam.

But she couldn't see into the shop to see what Mum and Tom were getting for her. So she looked at the Christmas trees. "Are there five trees as well, Sam?" she asked.

She started to count the trees in the window.

"One, two, three, four. I can only count four trees," she told Sam. "We have only got one tree at home, but it's a very nice tree. These trees have only yellow and orange balls on them. Our tree has red and blue and green balls as well. We like our tree, don't we, Sam?" she said.

Tom came out of the shop with a big present. Kate looked at it. She knew that if she asked Tom what the present was, he wouldn't tell her. So she didn't say anything.

Mum looked at Kate, "Have we been very long?" she asked.

"No, you haven't," Kate said. "I've been looking at Father Christmas and the trees in the window. I can count five presents and four trees. And Sam knew he had to be good, so he just sat and looked at the window with me. I told him all about it."

At the next shop, Mum told Tom to wait outside while Kate went in with her to get Tom's Christmas present. Kate knew what she wanted to buy for Tom — the police car and the police van. So she went in with her mum to buy them.

Now it was Tom's turn to look in the shop window. There were five angels. But they had only four books to sing from, so two angels had to sing from the same book. They were very happy angels.

Then Sam would not stop barking. Tom told him to stop and looked round. What he saw surprised him. Two men had come out of a bank and were running away up the street.

The tall man had a big bag and the little man had a little bag. They ran very fast up the street away from the bank. As the men ran, the tall man bumped into an old woman and his cap fell off. He bumped her quite hard and she fell over. Tom saw her as she fell over.

"Oh dear, oh dear, my arm," said the woman as she sat up. "That man hurt my arm when he bumped into me."

Then Tom saw a man from the bank go to help the woman. So he looked at the men as they ran up the street.

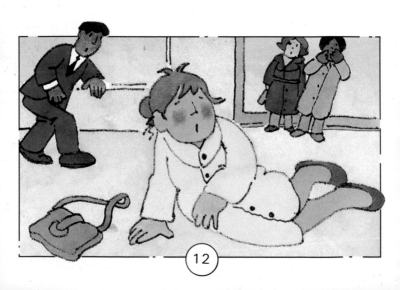

They got into a green car just past the bus. They went off very quickly up the street. Tom looked at the car going away.

Then he looked at Sam. He had got the tall man's cap.

"Oh, you are a good dog, Sam," Tom said. And Sam gave him the cap.

The woman who had been hurt had lots of help now. Two men put a jacket over her and another woman went to get help.

Then a policeman came and talked to the woman who had hurt her arm. He talked to the men round her. They said that they had not seen where the robbers went. Then he came over to talk to Tom by the shop window.

"Did you see where those men went?" he asked.

So Tom told him that they ran up the street, got into a green car and went off quickly. Then Tom said, "And this is the tall man's cap. It fell off." And he gave him the cap.

"Well done," the policeman said.

"It was Sam, really," Tom told him. "Sam got the cap off the street."

"Well done, Sam," said the policeman.

Tom told the policeman all about the robbers. Then he said to the policeman, "I know the number of the green car as well."

"Really?" asked the policeman. "What is it then?"

So Tom told him, ''TAK,'' and he gave him the number.

''How do you know it was TAK?'' the policeman asked.

Then Tom told him, ''Because, you see, TAK is Tom and Kate. That is my name and my sister's name. My sister is Kate.''

The policeman took out his pencil because he wanted to write everything down. But his pencil wouldn't write.

A policewoman came over to them and gave him her pencil. Then the policeman told her all about Tom.

"And Tom got the number of the getaway car," he told her.

"You did do well," the policewoman told Tom. "Where do you live?"

The policeman told Tom that he wanted to write down his name and address.

"Where do you live?" he asked. "I must write down your address."

Tom gave him his address. Then he told him about his mum, dad, his sister Kate and Sam.

Tom saw his mum and his sister coming. Mum was surprised to see Tom talking to a policeman and a policewoman. She asked, "What's the matter, Tom?"

The policeman told her about the bank robbers and how Tom had got the number of the getaway car.

Mum and Kate were surprised and Mum told Tom that he had done very well. So Tom told them about Sam and how he had got the tall robber's cap.

Then Mum looked at the woman who had been hurt. "That's Mrs Davis," she said, and she went over to see her.

"Hello, Mrs Davis. How did you get hurt?" Mum asked.

Mrs Davis told her about the tall robber who bumped into her so that she fell over and hurt her arm.

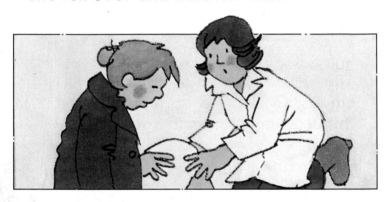

Just then the ambulance came down the road, and the ambulance men put Mrs Davis into the ambulance.

"We will come and see you in hospital, Mrs Davis," said Mum. "We will come and see you soon."

The ambulance went off quickly.

Tom was so pleased with himself that he didn't think of looking to see what Kate had got him for Christmas. If he had looked, he would just have seen the two boxes in his mother's bag. They went to the bus stop to wait for the bus to take them home.

When Dad came home from work, Tom told him all about the bank robbers and how the policeman was very pleased with him for getting the number of the getaway car. Then he told him how Sam got the tall robber's cap, and about the ambulance.

The next morning, Tom and Kate went with their mum to see Mrs Davis in hospital.

"Everyone has to be quiet in hospitals," Mum told them.

They left Sam at home as animals could not go into the hospital. On the way to the hospital they got some flowers for Mrs Davis.

"These anemones are so lovely," said Mum. "Mrs Davis should like these."

"But anemones live in the sea," Tom told her. "I've seen them in the sea."

"That's right," laughed Mum. "Those anemones do live in the sea, but these anemones are flowers. There are sea anemones and flower anemones."

They had to walk a long way in the hospital before they saw Mrs Davis. It was very quiet. She was sitting up in bed with a cup of tea. She had a big bandage on her arm.

"Hello, Mrs Davis," Mum said. "Are you all right?"

"Hello Jenny. Hello Kate. Hello Tom. It's lovely to see you all. I'm very well really, and it's nice and quiet here," Mrs Davis told them. "It's just my arm that still hurts. But it will be all right soon. Quite all right."

"So will you be home soon?" Mum asked Mrs Davis.

"Yes, I will be going home in two days," Mrs Davis told them. Then Tom gave her the anemones.

"What lovely anemones. They are nice. Thank you all very much," Mrs Davis said. "They can go in that vase over there."

Kate put some water in the vase. Tom took the paper off the flowers and put them in the water.

They told Mrs Davis how Sam had got the bank robber's cap. They told her how Tom knew the number of the getaway car. Tom told her how the policeman's pencil wouldn't write and he had to get a pencil from a policewoman.

Mrs Davis said that if the police knew all that, they should find the robbers quite quickly. She told Tom that he had done very well to get the number of the getaway car.

"First they will find the car, and then they will get the men," Mrs Davis said.

Then they said goodbye to Mrs Davis and she started to write some letters.

Tom asked his mum if Mrs Davis had a lot of letters to write.

"I think she will write to everyone who gave her flowers," said Mum. "And she had a lot of flowers as you could see."

"So she will have a lot of letters to write," Tom said.

EXIT▶

"What does E — X — I — T say?" asked Kate.

"EXIT," said Mum. "That is the way out of the hospital."

"So EXIT tells us which way to go?" asked Kate.

"That's right," Mum said. "This hospital is so big that we need to know how to get out and EXIT shows us where to get out." Mum said that it was time they went home to see Sam.

"He will need a walk by now and then he will need something to eat," she told them. "Let's see if we can get a bus quickly."

They went down the road to the bus stop. They had to wait for the bus.

While they waited, Kate asked her mum, "Will they take the bandages off Mrs Davis's arm soon?"

"Yes," said her mum. "Then it will be quite better."

Then they got on the bus.

Kate looked out of the window while Tom and Mum were talking. She looked at the cars and vans on the road. Then she saw a green car. Tom said that the robbers had a green car, so she looked at it. Then she saw the number on the car.

"TAK," she shouted. "TAK. That green car is the bank robbers' car."

Mum and Tom looked at her, then they looked down at the road. Everyone on the bus looked too.

"That's it," said Tom. "That's the car, all right."

"Is it really?" asked Mum. "Are you sure?"

"Yes, Mum. Look I can see the number and TAK, Tom and Kate," he said. "I am sure, Mum."

So Mum said that if he was really sure, they had better get off the bus and ring the police.

Mum told the police where they were and which way the green car had gone. And that Tom was sure that it was the robbers' car. Then they had to wait by the road for a police car to come and get them.

"I think Sam is going to have a long wait before he gets let out," said Mum.

The police car came down the road very quickly. The policeman got out of the car to talk to them. They knew him as he was the same policeman that they had seen before.

"Which way did the green car go?" he asked Kate.

Kate told him which road she saw the car going down. So they went down the same road, faster than all the other cars and vans. But the green car was not there. It had gone.

"Are you sure that it went down this road?" he asked Kate.

"Yes, I am sure," she told him.

"Let's see if the car has been left anywhere," the policeman said. "The men may live round here."

"Or they may have left the car while they went to the shops," Tom told them.

"Lots of children live round here too," said Kate. She could see some playing in their gardens.

"That green car could have been left anywhere," said Mum. "We should get back to let Sam out."

"We'll just take you along some roads round here, and then we'll take you home," the policeman told them.

29

So they went up and down the roads in the police car. Where had the bank robbers left their car? *(You know where it is, don't you?)*

But no one in the police car saw the green car the first time they went down the road. The next time they went down the road, just one of them saw the green car. And that was Kate.

"There it is," she shouted. "Over there, by that house. We can't see it very well because of that big black van. They must live in that house."

The police car went on down the road.

"Why are you going on?" asked Tom. "The green car was back there."

But the policeman was talking to the men at the police station.

"Just a minute," the policeman said to Tom.

"We have got the car, TAK. We want some more men out here, please. Then we can surprise them."

In four minutes the other cars had come.

"We must go home now," Mum told them. "We will only be in the way if we stay here."

"We want to see them get the robbers," Kate and Tom said.

But they had to get into the police car.

"We really must get home to the dog," Mum told the policeman.

"You will be back in about five minutes," he said.

The car went very quickly and soon they were home.

"Here you are," said the policeman. "That only took four minutes." They all got out of the car. "We will let you know if we get those men," he said. The police car left very quickly, making a lot of noise.

So Tom, Kate and Mum went in to see if Sam was all right. He was very pleased to see them, and jumped up to say hello. Kate let him out into the garden while Mum got his dinner ready. He was happy to have a run in the garden and very pleased when Tom gave him his dinner.

"Dad should be home in five minutes," Mum told them. "We did have an exciting time, didn't we?"

Then Dad came home. He was very wet as it had started to rain. Kate told him that she had found the getaway car and that the police were very pleased. She told him that they could not wait to see if the police found the men, as they had to get back to let Sam out. Then Tom told him all about the police cars going faster than all the other cars and vans. And how they made a lot of noise.

"You have had an exciting time, haven't you?" said Dad. "My work is often exciting, but it's never as exciting as that. And you found the getaway car, Kate. You are a good girl. Where was it left?" So Kate told him where she had found the getaway car.

"First Tom got the number of the car, then Kate found it. Haven't we got two fantastic children, Mum?" said Dad.

When Mum had the dinner ready, they all sat down to eat it.

Tom said, "The robbers went into the bank to get lots of money."

Dad said, "Yes, robbers often want to take lots of money."

The next morning, while Tom and Kate were playing a game, Sam was barking. He could hear a noise at the door. When Mum went to open the door, she found a strange man there with a bag. She was not going to let him in, but he said that he was from the bank. He asked if he had the right address. He wanted to see Kate and Tom, so Mum let him come in.

He sat down with Mum, Kate and Tom to talk about the bank robbers. Then the man from the bank told Kate and Tom that he was very pleased that they had been so sensible.

He was pleased too, that Tom had got the car number and that his sister had found the car for the police. Then he said, ''The police have got the bank robbers at the police station now. And that is because you are two very sensible children, who keep their eyes open all the time.''

When Dad came home, the man from the bank told him why he had come to see Kate and Tom.

Then the man from the bank told them about the money.

"It was all found," he said. "It was all found in their house. And it was because Tom and Kate were so sensible that the bank got all its money back." Then he went on, "So I have a present for Kate and Tom to say thank you from everyone at the bank to two sensible children."

He looked in his bag and took out two money boxes. He gave one box to Kate and the other box to Tom.

"And here is something for a very sensible dog," he said.

"My box is making a noise," Kate told them. "But it's not like the noise my doll makes."

"So is mine," said Tom.

"They are making a noise because they have some money in them," said the man from the bank. "Tomorrow you can buy something for Christmas, or you can keep the money in the box for another day," he said.

"Thank you very much," said Tom and Kate.

"Yes," said Mum. "It really is very nice of you to give them the presents."

So Tom had the green box and Kate had the blue box. When they looked at them, they found that their names were on the boxes, so that they would always know which was which.

"That was all very exciting," Mum said. "Now I have to get everything ready for Christmas, and we haven't got all the presents. We shall have to go to the shops again tomorrow."

"Do you think that we shall see some more bank robbers tomorrow?" Kate asked.

"Yes," said Tom. "I think tomorrow will be another exciting day."

"Tomorrow may be exciting, but we don't want bank robbers every day," Dad said.

"I'm sure that Sam likes exciting days, too," said Kate. "And it will be exciting when I'm an angel in the school play."

"Let's be sensible," said Mum. "We need some quiet days now. Christmas is always exciting and we need some quiet days before then."

So they had some quiet days and then they had a very exciting Christmas.

Words introduced in this book

Number of words....................................56

Count how many presents.

Count how many books.

Count how many angels.

LADYBIRD
READING SCHEMES

Ladybird reading schemes are suitable for use
with any other method of learning to read.

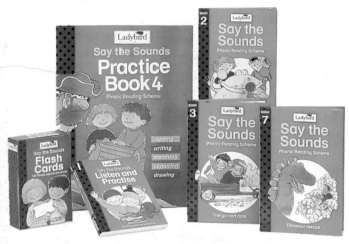

Say the Sounds

Ladybird's **Say the Sounds** graded reading scheme is a
phonics scheme. It teaches children the sounds of individual
letters and letter combinations, enabling them to tackle new
words by building them up as a blend of smaller units.

There are 8 titles in this scheme:

1 **Rocket to the jungle**   5 **Humpty Dumpty and the robots**
2 **Frog and the lollipops**   6 **Flying saucer**
3 **The go-cart race**   7 **Dinosaur rescue**
4 **Pirate's treasure**   8 **The accident**

Support material available: Practice Books, Double Cassette Pack,
Flash Cards